S0-ADF-465

From Gabby Fisher 12/93

PIERRE-AUGUSTE
Renoir

Paintings

WINGS BOOKS
New York • Avenel, New Jersey

Copyright © 1993 by Outlet Book Company, Inc.

All rights reserved.

This 1993 edition is published by Wings Books,
distributed by Outlet Book Company, Inc.,
a Random House Company,
40 Engelhard Avenue, Avenel, New Jersey 07001.

Random House
New York • Toronto • London • Sydney • Auckland

Grateful acknowledgment is made to Art Resource and Superstock
for permission to use their transparencies of the artwork.

Printed and bound in Malaysia

Library of Congress Cataloging-in-Publication Data

Renoir, Auguste, 1841-1919.
    Pierre Auguste Renoir : paintings.
        p.   cm.
    Includes bibliographical references.
    ISBN 0-517-09353-7
    1. Renoir, Auguste, 1841-1919 – Catalogs.   2. Impressionism (Art)-
-France. I. Title.
ND553.R45A4 1993
759.4 – dc20   93-1190
                                                                  CIP

8   7   6   5   4   3   2   1

"Believe me: it is possible to paint everything. To be sure, it is better to paint a pretty girl or a pleasing landscape. But anything can be a subject." [1]

—PIERRE-AUGUSTE RENOIR

1. *After Lunch* 1879

2. *Lise with a Parasol* 1867

3. *Portrait of Mlle. Irène Cahen D'Anvers* 1880

4. *Looking out at Sacre-Coeur* 1896

5. *A Large Vase of Flowers*

6. *Landscape in Algiers* 1881

7. *Mediterranean Fruits* 1881

8. *Portrait of Actress Jeanne Samary* 1878

9. *Portrait of Margot* c. 1878

10. *Road Climbing Through High Grass* 1875

11. *Moulin Huet Bay, Guernsey*

12. *Girl with a Hoop* 1885

13. *The Umbrellas* 1881-85

14. *Girl in a Boat*

15. *Claude Monet Reading*

16. *Young Girls at The Piano* 1892

17. *Vase of Roses*

18. *Madame Charpentier and her Children* 1878

19. *Dance in the Country* 1885

20. *Dance in the City* 1883

21. *The Seine at Asnieres*

22. *At "La Grenouilliere"* 1879

23. *The Bouquet*

24. *A Bouquet of Flowers*

25. *Gabriella with a Rose*

26. *Gabrielle with Jean* 1900

27. *Nude in a Chair*

28. *Two Bathers*

29. *Bathers*

30. *Woman with a Cat*

31. *The Lerolle Sisters*

Afterword

Pierre-Auguste Renoir, born in Limoges in 1841, grew up in the shadow of the Louvre and the Tuileries when his family moved to Paris in search of a better life. The son of a poor tailor, Renoir got a job as a painter of fine porcelain at the age of ten. As a young man, often on the brink of poverty, Renoir applied the skills he acquired in this job to other decorative work, embellishing fans, curtains, and moveable altars. The light brushstrokes, the delicate pinks, brilliant blues, and chrome yellow used in porcelain, and the pastoral scenes he reproduced on vases and plates, copied from the works of Watteau, Boucher, and other masters of the rococo, had an enduring effect on Renoir's artistic achievements. Renoir became a magician of light and color. In his paintings, "The light takes on material qualities, it foams and sparkles in his pictures, and sometimes illuminates the colors like precious stones."[2]

At twenty-one Renoir registered for courses at the Ecole de Beaux-Arts and joined other young artists—including Bazille, Sisley, and Monet—at the Gleyre Studio. Monet and Renoir quickly became known as revolutionaries among the students, as they overturned the canons of traditional art by rejecting its demands for "dignified" subject matter, balanced composition, precise drawing, and somber coloration. Following the lead of Courbet and Manet, they depicted the contemporary scene and, seeking to capture the certain Impressionist brush techniques, they are more carefully structured and more densely worked than his paintings of the previous decade. Inspired by the Raphael frescos he saw on a trip to Italy in 1881, Renoir began to work in a larger format and took renewed interest in the clarity of composition and the beauty of the line. *The Umbrellas* (plate 13), painted between 1881-5, shows Renoir in transition; while the figures on the right are strictly Impressionist in style, in those on the left Renoir emphasized the contrasts of rounded surfaces and the rigid edges of the objects. In *Dance in the City* (plate 20), executed in 1883, forms are clearly distinguished and the colors lack the vibrancy of Renoir's "pure" Impressionist paintings.

Hoping to create the "simplicity and grandeur" of Raphael's frescos, Renoir turned to the timeless themes of women and children. His future wife, a perfect example of the plump, rounded Renoir woman, served as a model for such paintings as *Dance in the Country* (plate 19). *The Bathers* (plate 29) represents the stylistic and artistic climax of this period. As Bruno F. Schneider writes, "The wonderful harmony of movement of the figures...is reminiscent of Classicist relief, and the many intersections of the legs of the two sitting girls are so balanced that they give the impression of belonging...to a choreographic study."[7] Renoir had returned to the studio to work, having come to believe, "An artist who paints straight from nature is really looking for nothing but momentary effects. He does not try to be creative and, as a result, the pictures soon become monotonous."[8]

This return to traditional painting techniques and the transition from the dominance of color to the dominance of line revitalized

Renoir's works. By the end of the 1880s, however, Renoir faced a more profound crisis. Attempting to reintroduce color while retaining his mastery of form, he often produced paintings that lacked the spontaneity and grace for which he is so admired. Slowly and painfully, Renoir emerged from this difficult period. In paintings like *Young Girls at the Piano* (plate 16) and portraits of his own children like *Gabrielle with Jean* (plate 26), his technique became softer and more painterly. Writing about the latter work, Renoir said, "One must be personally involved with what one does.... At the moment I am painting Jean pouting. It's no easy thing but it's a lovely subject."[9] Still-lifes of flowers and fruits provided Renoir with a respite from the demands of painting the human figure. "When I paint flowers," he told his friend Georges Riviere, "my mind has a rest.... I put different shades of color and try out some bold tonal values, without worrying about spoiling a canvas."[10]

Renoir's artistic crisis was ironically accompanied by public triumph. Successful exhibitions were held at the Durand-Ruel gallery in 1892 and in 1896, and in 1900, Renoir was made a *chevalier de la legion d'honneur*. International acclaim soon followed: 59 of his paintings were exhibited in London in 1905 and in 1907 the Metropolitan Museum of Art purchased *Madame Charpentier and her Children* for a vast sum of money.[11]

Even the rheumatism that crippled his hands at the turn of the century did not prevent Renoir from painting. His late works are almost classical in their beauty: quiet, simple, they glow with a richness that epitomizes Renoir's particular genius. On his small estate in Cagnes, Renoir turned his attention once again to the beauty of the nude female body. He told his son, Jean, "What I like is skin, a young girl's skin that is pink and shows she has good circulation. But what I like above all is serenity."[12] He continued to use a model, but "he scarcely looked at her; the visions appeared before his inner eye, and found their way onto the canvas."[13] Limiting himself to only a few colors, Renoir produced luminous portraits of women as he saw them in life: blooming, alive with the joy and the tasks of living, animated by a natural beauty as real and as eternal as nature itself.

Renoir's joy in painting remained to the end of his life; he was working on a painting of flowers when he died at Cagnes on December 3, 1919.

NOTES

1. Renoir's last words, quoted by Jean Renoir, *Renoir, My Father* (San Francisco: Mercury House, Inc.), 117
2. Bruno F. Schneider, *Renoir* (New York: Crown Publishers, Inc.), 6
3. Patrick Bade, *Renoir: The Masterworks* (New York: Portland House), 52
4. Schneider, p. 22
5. Jan Rewald, *The History of Impressionism* (New York: The Museum of Modern Art), 419
6. Schneider, 68
7. Ibid, 82
8. Bade, 26
9. Ibid, 126
10. Ibid, 34
11. Ibid, 36
12. Renoir, 104
13. Schneider, 88

List of Plates

The photographs in this book were supplied by:

COVER　　*By the Seashore*
　　　　　Metropolitan Museum of Art, New York
　　　　　Superstock, New York

BACK　　　*The Dance at the Moulin de la Galette*
COVER　　 Musée d'Orsay, Paris
　　　　　Erich Lessing/Art Resource, New York

TITLE　　 *Portrait of Auguste Renoir*
PAGE　　　By Frédéric Bazille
　　　　　Musée d'Orsay, Paris
　　　　　Giraudon/Art Resource, New York

PLATE 1　*After Lunch*
　　　　　Stadelisches Institute of Art, Frankfurt
　　　　　Superstock, New York

PLATE 2　*Lise with a Parasol*
　　　　　Folkwang Museum, Essen
　　　　　Erich Lessing/Art Resource, New York

PLATE 3　*Portrait of Mlle. Irène Cahen d'Anvers*
　　　　　Private Collection, Zurich
　　　　　Erich Lessing/Art Resource, New York

PLATE 4　*Looking out at Sacre-Coeur*
　　　　　Neie Pinakothek, Munich
　　　　　Superstock, New York

PLATE 5　*A Large Vase of Flowers*
　　　　　Fogg Art Museum, Cambridge
　　　　　Superstock, New York

PLATE 6　*Landscape in Algiers*
　　　　　Musée d'Orsay, Paris
　　　　　Art Resource, New York

PLATE 7   *Mediterranean Fruits*
           Art Institute of Chicago
           Superstock, New York

PLATE 8   *Portrait of Actress Jeanne Samary*
           Hermitage, St. Petersburg
           Scala/Art Resource, New York

PLATE 9   *Portrait of Margot*
           Louvre, Paris
           Giraudon/Art Resource, New York

PLATE 10   *Road Climbing Through High Grass*
           Musée d'Orsay, Paris
           Erich Lessing/Art Resource, New York

PLATE 11   *Moulin Huet Bay, Guernsey*
           National Gallery, London/Bridgeman Art Library
           Superstock, New York

PLATE 12   *Girl With a Hoop*
           National Gallery of Art, Washington, D.C.
           Superstock, New York

PLATE 13   *The Umbrellas*
           National Gallery, London
           Superstock, New York

PLATE 14   *Girl In a Boat*
           Private Collection
           Superstock, New York

PLATE 15   *Claude Monet Reading*
           Musée Marmottan
           Art Resource, New York

PLATE 16   *Young Girls at The Piano*
           Musée d'Orsay, Paris
           Erich Lessing/Art Resource, New York

PLATE 17   *Vase of Roses*
           Musée d'Orsay, Paris
           Scala/Art Resource, New York

PLATE 18   *Madame Charpentier and Her Children*
           Metropolitan Museum, New York
           Superstock, New York

PLATE 19   *Dance in the Country*
           Musée d'Orsay, Paris
           Erich Lessing/Art Resource, New York

PLATE 20   *Dance in the City*
           Musée d'Orsay, Paris
           Bridgeman/Art Resource, New York

PLATE 21   *The Siene at Asnieres*
           National Gallery, London
           Superstock, New York

PLATE 22   *At "La Grenouilliere"*
           Musée d'Orsay, Paris
           Erich Lessing/Art Resource, New York

PLATE 23   *The Bouquet*
           Superstock, New York

PLATE 24   *A Bouquet of Flowers*
           Israel Museum, Jerusalem
           Erich Lessing/Art Resource, New York

PLATE 25   *Gabriella with a Rose*
           Musée d'Orsay, Paris
           Scala/Art Resource, New York

PLATE 26   *Gabrielle with Jean*
           Musée Grenoble
           Scala/Art Resource, New York

PLATE 27   *Nude in a Chair*
           Museum of Fine Arts, Zurich
           Art Resource, New York

PLATE 28   *Two Bathers*
           Private Collection
           Scala/Art Resource, New York

PLATE 29   *Bathers*
            Louvre, Paris
            Giraudon/Art Resource, New York

PLATE 30   *Woman With a Cat*
            National Gallery of Art, Washington, D.C.
            Superstock, New York

PLATE 31   *The Lerolle Sisters*
            City of Bristol Museum
            Superstock, New York